Caitlin's Smile

W. T. Skye Garcia

Alfred

for Donna and Amanda

Caitlin's Smile

W. T. Skye Garcia

Tenderly, with expression (♩ = 104)

ped. simile

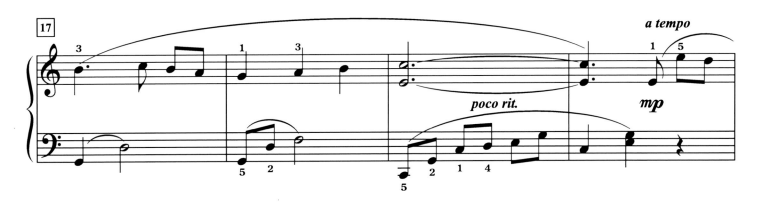

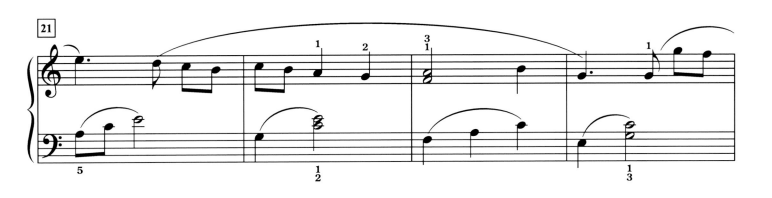

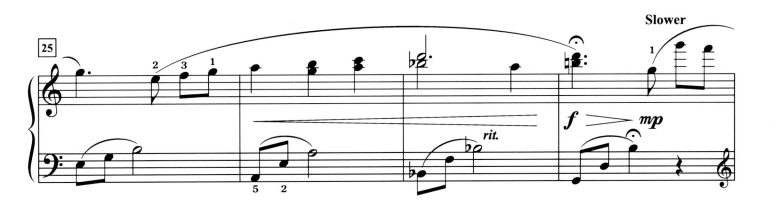

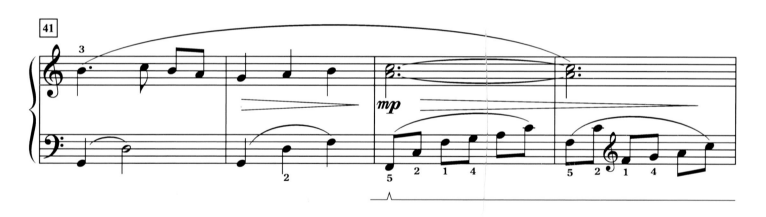

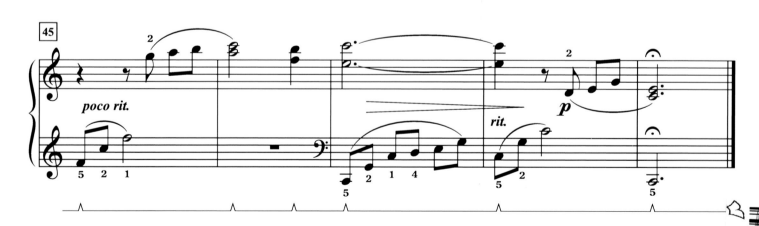

ISBN-10: 0-7390-6627-7
ISBN-13: 978-0-7390-6627-0

Alfred

alfred.com

34305 $3.99

ISBN 0-7390-6627-